Sedona
Arizona
Red Rock
Country
Tour Guide

By Waypoint Tours®

Front Cover - Cathedral Rock Reflections from Red Rock Crossing

Back Cover - Oak Creek Reflections at Slide Rock State Park

WAYPOINT TOURS®

Contents

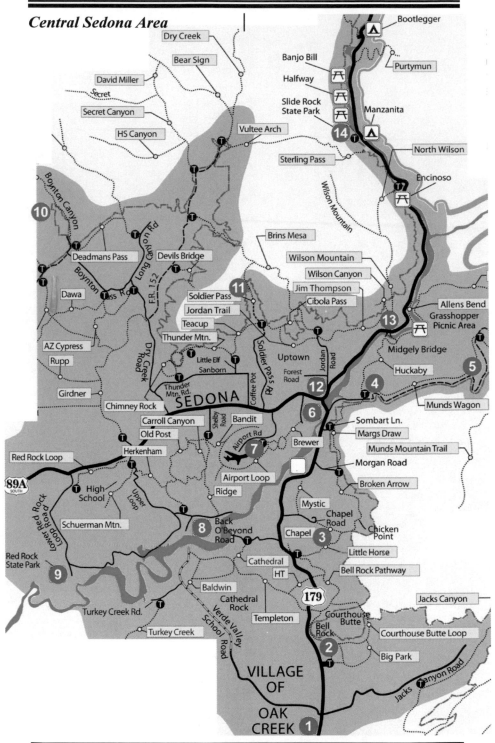

Central Sedona Area

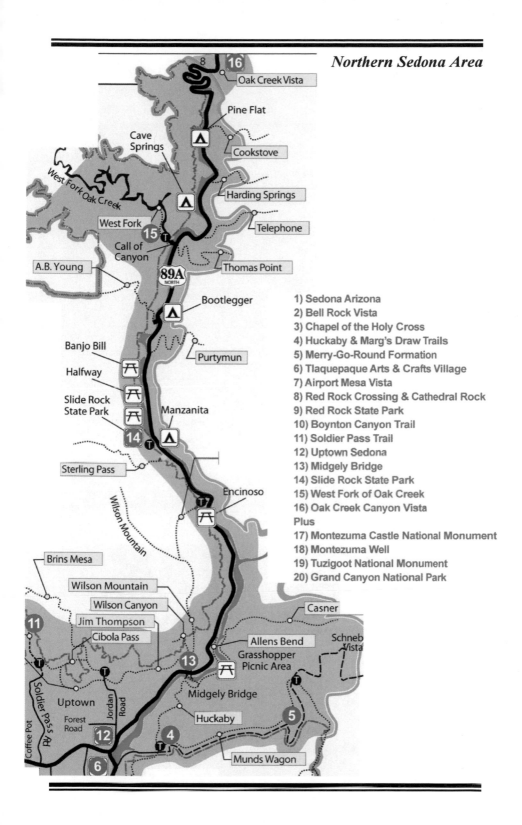

Oak Creek Vista

Pine Flat

Cave Springs

Cookstove

West Fork Oak Creek

Harding Springs

West Fork

Telephone

Call of Canyon

89A NORTH

A.B. Young

Thomas Point

Bootlegger

Banjo Bill

Purtymun

Halfway

Slide Rock State Park

Manzanita

Sterling Pass

Encinoso

Wilson Mountain

Brins Mesa

Wilson Mountain

Wilson Canyon

Casner

Jim Thompson

Schneb Vista

Cibola Pass

Allens Bend

Grasshopper Picnic Area

Soldier Pass Rd

Uptown

Coffee Pot

Forest Road

Jordan Road

Midgely Bridge

Huckaby

Munds Wagon

1) Sedona Arizona
2) Bell Rock Vista
3) Chapel of the Holy Cross
4) Huckaby & Marg's Draw Trails
5) Merry-Go-Round Formation
6) Tlaquepaque Arts & Crafts Village
7) Airport Mesa Vista
8) Red Rock Crossing & Cathedral Rock
9) Red Rock State Park
10) Boynton Canyon Trail
11) Soldier Pass Trail
12) Uptown Sedona
13) Midgely Bridge
14) Slide Rock State Park
15) West Fork of Oak Creek
16) Oak Creek Canyon Vista
Plus
17) Montezuma Castle National Monument
18) Montezuma Well
19) Tuzigoot National Monument
20) Grand Canyon National Park

Sedona Arizona Red Rock Country Tour Notes

1) Sedona Arizona
2) Bell Rock Vista
3) Chapel of the Holy Cross
   From 179 drive 1 mile east on Chapel Road
4) Huckaby & Marg's Draw
   From 179 drive east on Schnebly Hill Road to parking lot at end of pavement
5) Merry-Go-Round Formation (4-wheel drive, high-clearance vehicles only)
   From Huckaby & Marg's Draw continue 4+ miles east on rugged
   Schnebly Hill Road
6) Tlaquepaque Arts & Crafts Village
   Just south of the Y* on 179
7) Airport Mesa Vista
   From 89A drive south on Airport Road to any of 3 scenic overlooks
8) Red Rock Crossing & Cathedral Rock
   From 89A drive south on Upper Red Rock Road to Crescent Moon Ranch
9) Red Rock State Park
   From Red Rock Crossing continue south on dirt Upper Red Rock Road
10) Boynton Canyon Trail
   From 89A drive almost 3 miles north on Dry Creek Road until it ends,
   Drive west on Boynton Pass Road 1.5 miles,
   Drive north on Boynton Canyon Road to the nearby parking lot
11) Soldier Pass Trail
   From 89A drive 1.5 miles north on Soldier Pass Road,
   Drive east 0.2 miles on Rim Shadow Drive to the parking lot on the left
12) Uptown Sedona
13) Midgely Bridge
14) Slide Rock State Park
15) West Fork of Oak Creek
16) Oak Creek Canyon Vista

* The "Y" is the intersection of 89A & 179

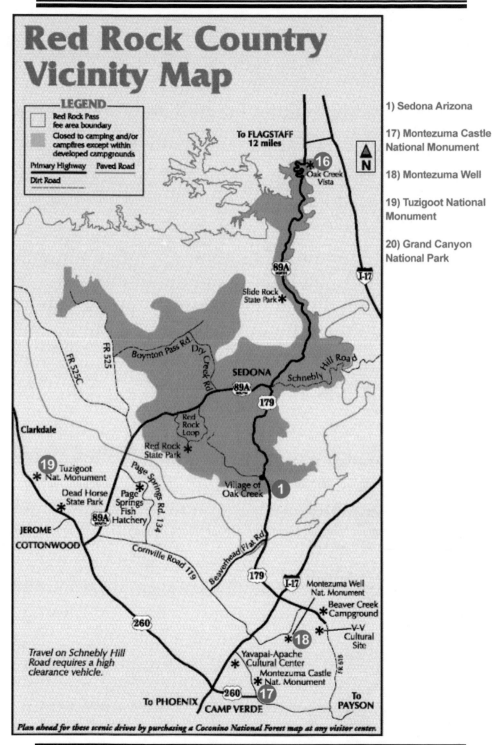

Red Rock Country Vicinity Map

LEGEND

- Red Rock Pass fee area boundary
- Closed to camping and/or campfires except within developed campgrounds
- Primary Highway — Paved Road
- Dirt Road

To FLAGSTAFF 12 miles

N

Oak Creek Vista — 16

89A

Slide Rock State Park

Boynton Pass Rd. — Dry Creek Rd.

FR 525C — FR 525

SEDONA — 89A

Schnebly Hill Road

179

Clarkdale

Red Rock Loop

Red Rock State Park

19 Tuzigoot Nat. Monument

Page Springs Rd. 134

Dead Horse State Park — Page Springs Fish Hatchery

89A

Village of Oak Creek — 1

JEROME
COTTONWOOD

Cornville Road 119

Beaverhead Flat Rd.

179

I-17 — Montezuma Well Nat. Monument

Beaver Creek Campground

V-V Cultural Site

18

260

FR 618

Yavapai-Apache Cultural Center

Montezuma Castle Nat. Monument

17

Travel on Schnebly Hill Road requires a high clearance vehicle.

260 — To PHOENIX — CAMP VERDE

To PAYSON

Plan ahead for these scenic drives by purchasing a Coconino National Forest map at any visitor center.

1) Sedona Arizona

17) Montezuma Castle National Monument

18) Montezuma Well

19) Tuzigoot National Monument

20) Grand Canyon National Park

1) Sedona Arizona

Welcome to Red Rock Country! Whether you have come to Sedona to golf, shop, hike, bike, and rock climb or just plain relax and enjoy the scenery, we hope this tour will enrich your Sedona experience. We'll introduce you to the story behind the magnificent scenery. You'll hear about early settlers, Native Americans, plants, rocks and animals of the region, and the forces of nature that created this unique place.

If you could look at the state of Arizona from above, you would see the red, salmon, and cream-colored rocks of Sedona lace the edges of the 3,000-foot high Mogollon rim. A serendipitous set of natural phenomena has created a striking landscape of spires, buttes, and canyons. Here, at the edge of the Mogollon Rim, the wide expanses of the Colorado Plateau in northeastern Arizona tumble down through a jumble of mountains and canyons, and smooth out into broad basins and northwest trending mountain chains in southern and western Arizona.

"Red Rock Country" may look familiar to you, even if you've never been here before. It is one of the most photographed spots in Arizona, and these formations were featured in classic western movies like "Angel and the Badman" with John Wayne, "Broken Arrow" with Jimmy Stewart and "Call of the Canyon," adapted from the novel written by Zane Grey.

Sedona is an unusual name for a town, but then, it was an unusual name for a baby. It's not Spanish, or Native American, but simply, American. Amanda Miller, a woman of Pennsylvania Dutch heritage living in Missouri, made up the name for her daughter because she thought it sounded pretty. On Sedona's 20th birthday in 1901, she married Theodore Carlton (Carl) Schnebly, who promptly took her to Arizona, where his brother Ellsworth was living.

Only five families lived in the area, and the new two-story Schnebly home was the one place large enough to accommodate guests, so it became the town's first hotel and general store. Carl Schnebly organized a post office, and submitted the names "Oak Creek Crossing" and "Schnebly Station" to the Postmaster General. Upon being told that they were too long for a postmark, Carl's brother suggested he name it after Sedona, and so the pretty place acquired a pretty name.

Left - Statue of Sedona Schnebly outside the Sedona Library
Bottom Right - Madonna & Praying Nuns viewed from the Chapel of the Holy Cross

2) Bell Rock Vista

Bell rock is one of the most famous and most easily recognized landmarks in "Red Rock Country." "The Rounders," a movie starring Henry Fonda and Glenn Ford, was filmed near Bell Rock. The producer, Richard Lyons, later said,

"Nowhere else did we find color quite as appealing as that of your red rock country. The sparkling color suits the mood of our film, which is a happy, hilarious modern western. It will be shown on wide-angle Panasonic because we don't want to miss any of this panoramic scenery."

The beautiful red color of Bell Rock and other landmarks in Sedona comes from a thin coating of red iron oxide on individual sand grains. The iron is only one-half of one percent of the rock's weight, but what a difference it makes!

Much of Sedona's dramatic scenery is carved from rock layers known as the Schnebly Hill Formation. They are unique to Red Rock Country. From the bright orange-red Rancho Rojo layer at the bottom, to the slightly darker Bell Rock layer, to the light-colored Fort Apache limestone and siltstone, each layer reflects the environment at the time the rocks were laid down. When the surfaces of the quartz sand grains are frosted, or covered with fine scratches, it shows they were once carried by wind rather than water.

The graceful curving terraces of the Bell Rock layer have ripple marks, which suggest this layer was deposited in a broad tidal zone. The gray Fort Apache was deposited in a shallow sea. It is only 10 – 12 feet thick here, but it is easy to spot between the red layers. Look for it near the top of Bell Rock and midway up on Courthouse Butte.

Looming above the Sedona Golf Resort in the Village of Oak Creek is House Mountain, a volcano that intrigues geologists. Lava flows extend in three directions, but not to the north. After investigation, they determined that the Mogollon Rim had blocked the northern lava flows 13 million years ago. Since then, the Rim has eroded back nearly four miles to the northeast, and the lake, which once filled this valley, has been gone for over two million years. It takes time to create something this beautiful!

Volcanoes and erosion aren't the only forces operating here. Some believe Sedona is one of the Earth's major power points of spiritual energy. Bell Rock's vortex is considered to have electric or masculine energy. Some visitors report feeling sudden power boosts and an emotional uplifting of the spirit. They feel compelled to climb the heights both physically and spiritually.

Below - House Mountain
Top Right - Bell Rock
Bottom Right - Courthouse Butte

3) Chapel of the Holy Cross

With so many dramatic rock forms, a chapel might be overlooked. But once the eye rests on the Chapel of the Holy Cross, it returns again and again. The pale angular building rises from the rocks, proudly displaying the cross as its focal point, both from within and without.

The road curves up the hill toward the chapel and suspended ramp walkways swoop up from the road to the church's entrance. The setting and the architecture convey a feeling of graceful motion. The vista from the terrace is remarkable. Bell Rock and Courthouse Butte are visible to the south and Cathedral Rock to the west. On the ridge to the east is a smaller rock spire known as "Madonna with Child" and two larger ones known as the "Praying Nuns."

The chapel is an inspiration, drawing from and adding to the beauty of Sedona. Inside, furnishings are simple in form. A myriad of red candles with flickering flames attracts attention briefly, but your gaze and soul are drawn to the large windows, the magnificent views through the glass, and the cross that supports and is supported by the building.

Marguerite Brunswig Staude first conceived her idea of a church with the cross as an integral part of the design while looking at the newly constructed Empire State Building. Lloyd Wright, son of famous architect Frank Lloyd Wright, was also influential in the design. Originally, the church was to be built in Budapest, overlooking the beautiful Danube River. However, fate and World War II intervened.

Marguerite hoped to find a new site for the church in her beloved Red Rock Country. A wonderful site was found, but it was on National Forest Service Land. Barry Goldwater came to the rescue and guided a bill through Congress, allowing the Chapel of the Holy Cross to be built in 1956.

The chapel is associated with the parish of St. John Vianny in Sedona. St. John Vianny, of Ars, France, was gifted with discernment of spirits, prophecy, and hidden knowledge. Thousands came to hear his sermons and for reconciliation, just as thousands visit the beautiful Chapel of the Holy Cross and experience an uplifting of their spirit.

4) Huckaby & Marg's Draw Trails

Marg's Draw Trail is named for an elusive Morgan horse owned by pioneer Abraham James. Marg must have figured out that new horseshoes meant an arduous journey to Camp Verde and Prescott, because after being reshod, the clever horse would disappear for a couple of days. However, eventually, Marg would always be found in the same spot, enjoying the shade and grass.

Many others have lingered here, enjoying the views, including early settlers, Hollywood film crews, hikers and sightseers. Marg's Draw was just one of many Sedona locations featured in the 1952 movie "Broken Arrow," in which Jimmy Stewart tries to keep peace between the Cochise Indians and the settlers.

Marg's Draw Trail leads to the Crimson Cliffs at the base of Munds Mountain to the east. Huckaby Trail, which heads north, was named after Jim Huckaby, who lived on a sandy flat near the stream crossing at Midgely Bridge. Huckaby Trail connects with the Jim Thompson Trail, and is a popular mountain biking as well as hiking trail. One biker's review called it a *"roller coaster single-track with short steep climbs and killer technical downhills. Don't look over the edge. Watch out for the waterbar staircase..."*

A short distance down the hill from the trailhead is the Sedona Schnebly Historical Home. Sedona is the pioneer for whom the city was named and she lived here with her husband in the 1920s and 30s. It is the only remaining home of the Schnebly couple. In 1995, their granddaughter, Lisa Schnebly Heidinger, posed as a model for a sculpture of Sedona Schnebly. The sculpture, created by Susan Kliewer, now stands in front of the Sedona Library.

The name of the canyon to the west, which Schnebly Hill Road follows, is Bear Wallow. Black bears are found in chaparral and pinyon pine forests throughout the uplands of Arizona. Their coats can be black, brown or even cinnamon in color, and they can weigh up to 400 pounds. Bears don't normally bother humans unless provoked or their cubs are in danger; but Richard Wilson, an old Arkansas bear hunter, was attacked by one. His boot, scarred with teeth marks, was later found near the tree the old hunter had tried to climb. He didn't make it. Apparently, the bear didn't either. Years later, the skeleton of a huge bear was found two miles away. Old-timers believe the bear died of a knife wound at the hand of Wilson. It had been a battle to the end between two tough adversaries.

The views along the drive from here to the Merry-Go-Round formation on the rugged, dirt Schnebly Hill Road are worth the effort and bumpy ride. If you are concerned about taking your own vehicle, you may want to opt for an even greater adventure as jeep tours often frequent this spot.

5) Merry-Go-Round Formation

Driving carefully up the rugged, dirt Schnebly Hill Road in your high-clearance 4x4 vehicle, you get an idea of what the early pioneers went through just to get from one place to the next. Since most of the road is still dirt and winds through uninhabited country, it's also not difficult to imagine driving a herd of cattle or a team of horses along it.

In the late 1890s, beef was in demand by miners in nearby Jerome. To fatten his cattle during the summer, Jim Mund herded thousands of them up the side of the mountain to higher elevations where they could graze on bunch grasses. The cowboys who drove them lived on beans, biscuits, an occasional peach, and $3 a day. Traces of their route can still be seen across the sandstone outcrops and through the oak and juniper.

Until 1902, the only other way to Flagstaff to purchase tools, food, and medicine was the stagecoach road which ran 11 miles south of Sedona. Traveling the 60-mile route took nearly a week. Pioneers like Carl Schnebly realized it would be shorter and more direct to follow Mund's trail up the mountain. Travel time could be cut to two days and produce would still be fresh when it arrived in Flagstaff.

J.J. Thompson got a $600 contract from the county for a small crew. Carl Schnebly and his brother Ellsworth helped complete the last ten miles of the steep route, using only picks, shovels, and dynamite. After it was built, Schnebly would take produce up the hill and bring lumber back. That's not how the road got its name, though. The Schnebly home happened to be at the end of the road.

It's easy to see how the Merry-Go-Round, one of the most prominent formations on this road, got its name. Apache limestone forms the round base, while the softer Schnebly Hill sandstone has eroded into whimsical animal shapes. Park and climb to the top at the backside of the Merry-Go-Round and enjoy the impressive views. Hear the wind whistle in the juniper and pines; see the red rock formations rise in sharp contrast against the deep purple-blue of the horizon. Off to the west look for Teapot Rock, Mitten Ridge, Thumb Butte and Moose's Butte. You'll also see flat rust-colored rock slabs called "Cow Pies." "Angel and the Badman," with John Wayne, was shot around these strange formations. Another movie filmed here was "Johnny Guitar" with Joan Crawford and Sterling Hayden.

If your eyes are sharp and the air is clear, you may even see all the way to the historic mining town of Jerome, where the beef that once roamed these hills was taken. Look for the mine tailings on the long mountain ridge forming the south side of the Verde Valley.

6) Tlaquepaque Arts & Crafts Village

Tlaquepaque is a place that not only sells art, but also is a work of art itself. It is named after a picturesque suburb of Guadalajara, Mexico's Queen City. Abe Miller, a visionary businessman, spared no expense in emulating the methods and styles of Mexican artisans. To help his crews better express the essence of Tlaquepaque, he took his architects and construction workers to Old Mexico for inspiration.

As a result, Sedona's Tlaquepaque has Mexican charisma, but also embraces modern art. Visitors love to wander the four different courtyards and narrow passages. Arches, fountains, niches, colorful tile, flowers, and birds combine in an ambiance that soothes and enchants. The large trees, which have grown on the banks of Oak Creek for hundreds of years, add to the charm. Abe built around the historic cottonwoods and not one was cut down.

The cottonwoods are the ones with the shaggy bark and shimmering, shaking leaves similar to an aspen, but the trees are considerably larger, growing up to 100 feet tall and 5 feet in diameter. The female trees produce tiny seeds that drift through the air with cotton-soft parachutes for which the trees were named.

Sycamores are the large trees with white and tan patchwork on their trunks. Their seeds are contained within woody, prickly balls, and their leaves, which turn golden yellow in the fall, look like maple leaves on steroids.

Sedona's second settler, Abraham James, built his cabin at this beautiful site in 1879. In the early 1900s, this was the location of Schnebly's Hotel and General Store. Now Los Abrigados Resort is here and guests are still welcome.

Come at Christmas time and enjoy a spectacular light show at Los Abrigados. From mid-November through early January, the resort is decorated with more than a million lights. Fifty families are selected from among hundreds of applicants to design holiday light displays. Visitors vote for their favorite. Dancing lights, Christmas music, cider, roasted chestnuts, carolers, carriage rides, and Santa add to the holiday magic called Red Rock Fantasy.

7) Airport Mesa Vista

The Airport Mesa is said to give elevating and inspiring energy. At this vortex the views are definitely uplifting. A trail leads from Airport Road to a ridge of vermillion sandstone eroded into smooth shapes. From the top, you'll have a fantastic 360 degree panorama of Sedona and the Red Rock area. On cloudy days, you may see the mist banked against the Mogollon Rim, making the colors richer with moisture and adding even more drama to the landscape.

Another viewpoint, near the crest of the hill, has spectacular views at sunset of many landmarks. If you consider north to be at 12:00, Chimney Rock is at 10 o'clock. The mountain behind it is called Capitol Butte. The Sphynx is at 1:00. Look for Coffeepot Rock at about 11 o'clock. It looks like the ones cowboys used on their campfires, and sometimes even glows as if the setting sun were freshly brewing it.

In 1945, Republic Pictures constructed a small frontier town movie set near Coffeepot Rock for "Angel and the Badman." It was used in several films, but was torn down to make way for a residential subdivision called Sedona West. The names of the movies are recorded in the street names: Pony Soldier Road, Flaming Arrow Way, Johnny Guitar Drive, and Last Wagon Drive. They are a lasting legacy of an unusual period in Sedona's history.

To the northwest is Boynton Canyon where ancient Indian ruins are found, along with a large vortex containing balanced energy. Perhaps ancient Indians had discovered its secret. Projectile points found in Arizona date back to around 10,000 B.C. and indicate that early man hunted camels, elephants and saber-tooth tigers that also lived here at that time. Although hunting and gathering remained part of Indian life, about 2,000 years ago a shift was made to agriculture and irrigated crops. The Sinagua People, whose name means "without water," found streams and food here; acorns, pinyon nuts, walnuts, sunflower seeds, berries, yucca fruit, leaf greens, mesquite pods, cactus fruit and agave were just a few of the items on nature's menu.

From 1130 to 1300 A.D., Indians lived in pit houses and later in cliff dwellings during the Honanki Phase. Artifacts indicate that this was a major crossroads for trading shells from the Pacific Coast, parrot feathers from South America and turquoise from Arizona.

A break in the historical record occurs around 1425 A.D. Drought, disease, and warfare have all been suggested, but no one really knows what happened. When the Spanish arrived, they found Yavapai Indians living here. Although the cavalry drove the Indians from this region, many are now returning to teach the new residents to love and respect this beautiful land.

8) Red Rock Crossing & Cathedral Rock

The majestic rock formation called Cathedral Rock rises above lovely Oak Creek. The contrast of blue water, lush green vegetation, and red rock is breathtaking. Over 75 movies have been made in Red Rock Country and film makers love this spot in particular. It was featured as a backdrop in many of the old westerns of the 1940s and 50s. Look for it next time you watch "Blood on the Moon" with Robert Mitchum.

Despite its name, the only crossing here now is a seasonal footbridge. A 20-mile drive separates the vistas on each side. Nevertheless, it has been a popular spot for a long time. Indian groups gathered and hunted food along the stream for thousands of years.

John H. Lee came around 1876 and homesteaded the land. He built the first irrigation ditch, brought in some cattle, and called his place the OK Ranch. In the early 1900s, the area's first school was located near here. It wasn't until the 1930s that a crossing was constructed using concrete slabs at water level. The extreme flooding in 1978 completely wiped out the crossing.

In 1980, the ranch, now called the Crescent Moon, was sold to the U.S. Forest Service who created the day-use area. You'll find wide smooth paths and benches for quiet contemplation. From the water wheel, built around 1940, the trail follows an old irrigation ditch and ends at a vortex near the shore. The waters of Oak Creek are believed to have healing qualities, with the most powerful being at the base of Cathedral Rock.

Cathedral Rock, which can be seen to the east, has a relaxing, peace inducing, magnetic, or female vortex for those who need relief from stress. This area wasn't always so peaceful, however. Several basalt "dikes" show that hot molten lava once rushed through cracks and fractures on its way to the surface. Look for the gray protrusion centered below the towering red rocks as evidence of this activity.

Today's activities at Red Rock Crossing include swimming and fishing in the trout-stocked stream. Many come, however, simply to enjoy the spectacular view, particularly as the sunsets. Just when you think the show is over and Cathedral Rock is drenched in shadow, the alpenglow illuminates the spires in radiant light once again.

9) Red Rock State Park

Not only will you enjoy the trails and scenery of beautiful Red Rock State Park, you'll come away knowing more about the animals and plants of the Southwest. Don't miss the excellent displays in the Visitor's Center before starting out to explore the park firsthand.

In the Southwest, most wildlife is found near moving water, so Kisva and Smoke Trails, which lead through riparian areas, are good bets for wildlife sightings. Rare black hawks, mountain lions and javelina are all visitors and mule deer are seen regularly. Also, look for their telltale tracks. Javelina and mule deer tracks are made with sharp hooves. Coyote tracks look similar to a dog's, but mountain lion footprints are more rounded and don't show the retractable claws. Javelina, which look like skinny pigs, travel in groups of eight to twelve, sleeping, eating and playing together.

Eagle's Nest and Coyote Ridge Trails climb to the high points in the park with great vistas along the way. They lead through pinyon and juniper woodlands.

Pinyon pine is a compact tree with a short, crooked trunk and needles in clusters of two. It is the most drought resistant of all the pines in Arizona. It's delicious seeds, favored by birds, animals and humans, are known as pine nuts, Christmas nuts, Indian nuts, pignolias and pinons.

Several varieties of juniper grow in the Southwest; most are 20-40 feet high with shaggy bark and scale-like leaves. The berries are popular with birds and other wildlife, but only humans use them for flavoring gin! An ethno-botany guide, available at the Visitor Center, explains other traditional uses for the plants found along the trails. For a different experience, try a moonlight hike, usually offered on summer full moon nights.

In the 1940s, Jack and Helen Frye owned this land. Jack was the founder and former president of TWA Airlines. Falling in love with the place, the couple named their 286 acres Smoke Trail Ranch. They built a large rock house, called Apache Fire, with the help of Native Americans. The Arizona State Parks Board acquired the property in 1986 and opened it in 1991 for everyone to enjoy. Before you leave, be sure to check out the rooftop of the Visitor's Center for a great view of Cathedral Rock.

Bottom Right - Apache Fire Rock House on Smoke Trail Ranch

10) Boynton Canyon Trail

Could the beauty of Boynton Canyon be one of the reasons the Sinagua Indians chose to settle here? This canyon contains some of the best-preserved cliff dwellings in the Sedona area. Remnants of stone walls held together with clay mortar are sheltered in red rock alcoves high up on the canyon walls. The National Forest Service recommends viewing them from a distance and following the rules in the included Archaeological Site Etiquette Guide.

Short side trails off the main path often dead end in a circle of rocks. Although Native Americans still seek solace within the canyon, these are more likely the remnants of modern visitors who believe this canyon is a vortex that channels the earth's energy.

According to Yavapai legend, the first people lived in the ground at Montezuma Well. When it became flooded, first woman was saved by placing her in a wooden vessel that rose to the surface. Guided by a bird companion and protected by the powers of the white stone she carried, she was lead to Boynton Canyon, where she lived and eventually gave birth to a daughter she conceived with the Spirit of the Sun.

It is the unique geologic structure of the canyon that created conditions favoring population by fruitful plants, animals, and people, as well as contributing to the canyon's beauty. The differential weathering of the Schnebly Hill formation rocks results in sheer cliffs which shade the canyon floor, and the recessed alcoves where animals and humans can be warmed in the winter and sheltered from the hot summer sun. Intermittent flowing water carves the canyon and decorates the walls with curtains of desert varnish.

Succulents, like prickly pear cactus and yucca, and transition zone manizanita shrubs and alligator bark juniper, which are distributed along the canyon's length and breadth, provide an abundance of food. Today's Enchantment Resort is believed to be located where the Indians once farmed, and where early settlers homesteaded.

The oasis of beauty and plenty continues to attract a variety of not only birds and animals, but also people: from archeology buffs, to new wave enthusiasts; from ornithologists and naturalists, to tennis enthusiasts and resort relaxers.

Bottom Right - Enchantment Resort View

11) Soldier Pass Trail

The journey along Soldier Pass Trail, while always magnificent, has not always been as tranquil as it is today, with the elegant homes nestled in the shadows of Coffee Pot Rock and the Sphinx and the slackened water of the Seven Sacred Pools. The formation of the pools themselves required the turmoil of pebbles being trapped and swirled around and around in the intermittent stream's current. Eventually, the energy of the swirling pebbles eroded potholes in the bedrock of the stream and created catch basins to retain life-giving water in an otherwise summer parched landscape.

One reason the creeks in this area are generally dry is because the water flows through subterranean channels carved in the limestone layers, rather than on the surface. Sometimes the roof of these subterranean caves falls in and creates sinkholes such as the "Devil's Kitchen," seen less than a quarter mile from the trailhead. "Devil's Kitchen," the largest sinkhole in Sedona at over 100 feet across and more than 50 feet deep, was formed with a cataclysmic earth-shaking boom in the 1880s, which created a cloud of dust that hung suspended over the valley.

The bit of jarring and dust experienced by modern day jeep tour adventurers may be but a hint of the experiences of the Camp Verde Calvary who once used this trail to cross Soldier Pass between Brinn's Mesa and Capital Butte to access the cooler, game-enriched upper Dry Creek Canyons. Traveling up out of the canyons to higher elevations such as the Mogollon Rim in those days was no simple journey. The descriptions of Martha Summerhay's life as a calvary lieutenant's wife in her book, *Vanished Arizona* may help quench the thirst of those who wonder what it was really like back then:

The scenery was wild and grand; in fact, beyond all that I had ever dreamed of; more than that, it seemed so untrod, so fresh somehow, and I do not suppose that even now, in the day of railroads and tourists, many people have had the view of the Tonto Basin which we had one day from the top of the Mogollon range.

I remember thinking as we alighted from our wagons and stood looking over into the basin, "Surely I have never seen anything to compare with this – but oh! Would any sane human being voluntarily go through with what I have endured on this journey in order to look upon this wonderful scene?"

Top Right - Devil's Kitchen
Bottom Right - Seven Sacred Pools

12) Uptown Sedona

With such stunning natural landscapes, it's no surprise that artists, writers and musicians, some of international acclaim, are naturally drawn to Sedona. As a well-known destination for artists and art connoisseurs, Sedona has become a drive-through gallery with sculptures displayed outside many showrooms. With this much to see on the outside, just imagine the treasures inside the amazingly beautiful and unique galleries.

It all began with Egyptian artist Nassan Gobran who created the Sedona Arts Center in 1958 with the help of other visionaries, such as German surrealist Max Ernst. In 1965, Joe Beeler, Charlie Dye, John Hampton, and George Phippen met at the Oak Creek Tavern to charter the Cowboy Artists of America. The number of people in Sedona has more than tripled since then, and so has the art! As you stroll along the galleries and shops, benches, flowers and views are plentiful; relax and enjoy the scenery of Sedona.

To the northwest are Wilson Mountain, with its volcano, and Steamboat Rock, with its bridge of purple-gray Apache limestone. To the northeast are Teapot Rock, Thumb Butte, and Moose's Butte. To the southeast are Camel Head, Munds Mountain, and Snoopy. Do you see Lucy above the snoozing Snoopy?

Sedona dining experiences are also wonderful, with something for every palate: Mexican, Southwestern, American and Cowboy, to be sure, but there is French, Italian and Japanese as well. More shops, parking and views are found on Jordan Road that veers off Hwy 89A and heads up the hill. Continue along Jordan Road and you'll come to the new Sedona Heritage Museum at Jordan Historical Park. It's a great place for kids and has a picnic area, nature trail, and orchards. At the museum, you'll gain an appreciation for the challenges early pioneers and cowboys faced. You can also relive the heyday of Western movies as you discover more about the ones filmed here in the heart of "Red Rock Country."

Movies, commercials, music videos, and television documentaries are still being filmed in Sedona and the surrounding area. Movies that feature epic cross-country journeys often stop in Sedona, including the opening scenes of "Karate Kid" (1985), "Midnight Run" starring Robert DiNiro (1988), and a real classic, "National Lampoon's Vacation" with Chevy Chase (1983). The famous "Jazz on the Rocks" and other excellent concerts keep the stars, and the red rocks, in the spotlight. Look around you; you never know who might be strolling through the galleries of Sedona!

Below - Sedona Heritage Museum on Jordan Road
Top Right - Snoopy Rock with Lucy High Above

13) Midgely Bridge

The location of Uptown Sedona was originally determined by how far a wagon could make it up the valley. When J.J. Thompson built a four-mile long wagon road to his home in 1887, he also constructed ten creek crossings, which promptly washed away the next year. J. J. Thompson, Sedona's first settler, led an exciting life. He was born in Scotland in 1844 and immigrated to the United States at age 19. After spending time in Texas and fighting in the Civil War, the lure of rich land led him to Oak Creek. Here he discovered the corn, squash, and beans that Native Americans had planted, and so named his homestead, "Indian Gardens."

Not until 1901 did the road extend all the way through the canyon. The first bridge was built at Slide Rock in 1914 and washed away a few years later. By 1935, a wood bridge was constructed deep in Wilson Canyon along with a two-lane paved road. Finally, W.W. Midgely, a county supervisor, rounded up funds to shorten the route and span the Wilson gorge in 1939. As thanks for his efforts, the bridge was named for him. If you take the trail down into the canyon, you can still see remains of the old road and bridge.

You'll also find some of Sedona's oldest rocks. 350 million years ago, this spot was near the western coastline of North America, beneath a warm shallow sea where corals and other marine life abounded. After millions of years, these coral reefs became the Red Wall limestone, visible below Midgely Bridge and west of Sedona. Sedona's sinkholes, which form in limestone, have been given unusual names, such as "Devil's Kitchen" and "Devil's Dining Room."

Above the Red Wall limestone are the many layers of the Supai Formation, deposited 285 to 320 million years ago, before the age of dinosaurs, when amphibians and reptiles were just beginning to emerge onto land. The large sea had retreated, leaving a low, coastal flood plain between two smaller seas. As seas advanced and retreated repeatedly, the types of rocks being deposited changed with the sea level. The resulting complex collection of limestones, sandstones, mudstones, and conglomerates may be similar to rocks that are forming in other parts of the world today, like the seaside deserts of Saudi Arabia.

14) Slide Rock State Park

In addition to looking beautiful, the sandstone of Sedona and Slide Rock State Park weathers into smooth surfaces that are wonderful for water slides. One popular chute in the creek bottom is 30 feet long. What a cool thrill to shoosh through into the pool below. Try it; you'll feel like a kid again. Boulders and natural stone benches make great places to sit and dangle your toes in the creek or have a picnic.

The stream runs by the Pendley Homestead where Frank claimed squatter's rights in 1907. Perhaps because the Pendleys were from Texas, the barn resembles the Alamo. They watered the land with an irrigation system of tunnels and flumes that is still in use. In warm months, the family farmed; but come winter, Frank headed to southern Arizona to work in the mines. In 1912, he planted an orchard with many varieties of apple trees. It was one of the many orchards which contributed to Sedona's excellent reputation for fresh fruit, even as far away as Seattle, San Francisco and St. Paul. Delicious apples are still grown in the park and are available in season.

Apples weren't the only Pendley business; the tourist cabins are from the 1930s when this was a favorite honeymoon destination. "Gun Fury," the 1953 romance about a civil war veteran searching for his fiancée who had been kidnapped by outlaws, starring Rock Hudson and Donna Reed, is one of several westerns filmed here.

Slide Rock and the Pendley Homestead are truly four-season destinations. Come taste the apples and view the colors of autumn, see the contrast of white snow on red rocks in winter, smell the frothy white apple blossoms of spring and slide through the water chutes on a hot summer afternoon.

15) West Fork of Oak Creek

If you are looking for a place to experience Red Rock Country with all of your senses, try West Fork. Listen to water music as you cross the bridge. Feel the breeze as you go under the shade of the trees. Smell the refreshing aroma of leaves and pine needles. Wildflowers such as the blue violet and white Canadian violet, yellow butterweed, white candytuft and rockcress bloom in the spring beneath flowering apple, chokecherry, sycamore and Arizona alder trees. Snowberry, arroyo willow and dogwood shrubs add to the show. Even without spring blooms, some say this is the most beautiful side canyon.

Zane Grey, the famous Western writer, stayed in a hunting cabin here and wrote his novel, *Call of the Canyon*. In 1923, it was the first movie to be filmed in Sedona. A spectacular flash flood was an unexpected addition to the film.

One of the camera crew, Carl Mayhew, enjoyed his visit so much he returned in 1925 and built a lodge. Clark Gable, Susan Hayward, Cesar Romero, Jimmy Stewart, Maureen O'Hara, and Walt Disney were a few of the movie stars and producers who stayed at Mayhew's Lodge. President Herbert Hoover, Lord Halifax and other celebrities also relaxed in the peaceful canyon. The lodge burned down in 1980 before the U.S. Forest Service could renovate it. Today, vines cover tumbled-down walls, an arch, and a round window, creating a secret garden of green mystery.

Across the apple orchard, you have views of the white cliffs of Kaibab limestone on top of the Toroweap Formation. The division of the two upper layers from those underneath is the "green line." Pines and manzanita grow along a bench between the white Toroweap and the golden Coconino sandstone beneath. Coconino sandstone is easily identified by the sweeping lines of a former sand dune desert that extended from here to the Grand Canyon and beyond. The lowest, and therefore oldest, rocks seen here are the red rocks of the Schnebly Hill Formation, deposited at the fringes of the Pedregosa Sea.

If you were standing here at the time the Toroweap rocks were formed, you would be at the very edge of the sea - water to the west and land to the east. In the west, the Toroweap layer is limestones and other carbonates as would be deposited in a shallow sea. To the east, the rock is sandy quartz as would be deposited on coastal plains.

Millions of years later, Oak Creek Canyon developed along a fault, with the east side dropping down 700 feet, further differentiating the rocks on either side of the creek. The West Fork, however, developed along joints in the rock. With joints, the rock layers do not shift relative to each other, but still create a weak point for erosion to occur rapidly. The right angle zigzags of the West Fork slot canyon follow the pattern established by the joints deep into the Secret Mountain Wilderness. As you turn each bend on the trail along the stream, drink in the beauty of the cream and terra cotta colored rocks reflected in the quiet pools.

16) Oak Creek Canyon Vista

This lovely spot among the pines has wonderful views of Oak Creek Canyon. Native Americans from northern Arizona often have jewelry and other Indian crafts for sale - true Southwest souvenirs.

At the overlook, you can see some of the switchbacks of the road as they plunge down into Oak Creek Canyon. The 15 mile journey through the canyon is what some might call an "Oh, My!" road, both for the spectacular views and for the sheer descents. Flagstaff is at 7,200 feet; Sedona is at 4,400 feet.

As the elevation changes, so do the temperature, plants and animals. Flagstaff is about 10 degrees cooler than Sedona, and gets 10-15 more inches of precipitation. On top of the Mogollon Rim, you'll find ponderosa, white fir and Douglas fir; as you drop in elevation into Oak Creek Canyon, you will find chaparral shrublands consisting of scrub oak, manzanita and juniper. Scrub oak is more formally known as Turbinella oak, after the acorns that resemble little toy tops. Other species of oak which grow here, and help give the canyon its name, include Emory oak with shiny yellowish-green leaves that resemble holly, Gambel oak which has lobed leaves and a proliferous root system, and Arizona white oak, which hybridizes easily. Manzanita means little apples, and is named for the small yellowish-white/reddish-brown berries that are found among the twisted, mahogany-hued branches and small waxy leaves. Many animals, including skunks, coyotes, foxes, grouse, quail, bears and deer, enjoy these berries.

At the lowest elevations, you'll find prickly pear cactus, yucca, and desert dwellers such as coyotes, jackrabbits and lizards. Along the stream you'll find water-loving willows, sycamores and cottonwoods. Over 150 species and subspecies of birds have been recorded here due to the diverse habitat. For example, the pygmy nuthatch prefers the pine forests, whereas the red-breasted nuthatch prefers conifers and the white-breasted nuthatch prefers deciduous trees such as the cottonwoods and sycamores. A curious fact about nuthatches is they forage by traveling down tree trunks. That way they find bugs that other birds, such as woodpeckers, traveling up might have missed.

Not everything that flies is a bird, however. Bats are known to nest near the overlook; their favorite perches are old bridges and buildings, trees, and abandoned mines. When you consider that, in one night, a large colony of bats can eat up to 500,000 pounds of insects; you might want to keep them around. They hibernate in the winter and that seems essential for their survival. Please respect their privacy. Young, inexperienced bats may lose their grip and fall if startled, so let sleeping bats hang.

From this high vantage point, you may feel as if you are flying too. Oak Creek Canyon and beautiful Sedona are a land of contrasts; from scenic mountainous vistas to deep, cool canyons; from cozy bed and breakfast inns to spacious resorts with all the amenities; from Cowboy art to surrealism; from soothing to energizing vortexes; from desert dwellers to riparian habitat; and from ancient seas to modern day rocks, which provide the most striking contrast of all - the vibrant red buttes and spires silhouetted against rich green vegetation and verdant blue skies.

17) *Montezuma Castle National Monument*

Gaze through the windows of the past into one of the best-preserved cliff dwellings in North America. This 20 room high-rise apartment, nestled into a towering limestone cliff, tells a 1,000-year-old story of ingenuity and survival in an unforgiving desert landscape. Marveling at this enduring legacy of the Sinagua culture reveals a people surprisingly similar to ourselves.

On December 8, 1906, President Theodore Roosevelt celebrated the passage of the Antiquities Act by declaring four sites of historic and cultural significance as our nation's first national monuments. Among these was Montezuma Castle, which the President identified as a place "of the greatest ethnological value and scientific interest." Although very few original artifacts remained in the structure due to intensive looting of the site, Roosevelt's decision assured the continued protection of one of the best-preserved prehistoric cliff dwellings in North America.

Montezuma Castle National Monument quickly became a destination for America's first car-bound tourists. In 1933, "Castle A", a 45-50 room, pueblo ruin was excavated, uncovering a wealth of artifacts and greatly enhanced our understanding of the Sinagua people who inhabited this riparian "oasis" along Beaver Creek for over 400 years.

Early visitors to the monument were allowed access to the structure by climbing a series of ladders up the side of the limestone cliffs. However, due to extensive damage to this valuable cultural landmark, public access of the ruins was discontinued in 1951.

Now, approximately 350,000 people a year gaze through the windows of the past during a visit to Montezuma Castle. Even 600 years after their departure, the legacy of the Sinagua people continues to inspire the imaginations of this and future generations.

18) *Montezuma Well*

Montezuma Well, a unit of Montezuma Castle, is located 11 miles from the park. Formed long ago by the collapse of a limestone cavern, over one million gallons of water a day flows continuously into the well. This constant supply of warm, fresh water provides an aquatic habitat like no other in the world, and has served as an oasis for wildlife and humans for thousands of years.

The legacy of the Sinagua culture surrounds you during a visit to Montezuma Well. From cliff dwellings perched along the rim to large pueblo ruins and an ancient pit house, the variety of these archeological sites is a testament to the ingenuity of these people.

Take your time as you explore the trails at Montezuma Well and discover the tranquility of a site still considered sacred by many local tribes. The shaded forest along the trail near the swallet ruin and the outlet provides welcome relief from the unrelenting Arizona sunshine.

The temperature difference at the outlet can be up to 20 degrees cooler than along the rim of the well, making it easy to imagine the people of the Sinagua culture spending the hot summer days in this tranquil setting.

The constant supply of warm, 74-degree water was the life-blood of the people who made their home here. Over 1.5 million gallons of water flows into the well every day, a rate that has not fluctuated measurably despite recent droughts throughout the state of Arizona. This water enters a "swallet" near the end of the trail into the well and flows through over 150 feet of limestone before re-emerging from the outlet into an irrigation ditch on the other side. Sections of this ditch date back over 1,000 years. The value of this water is still recognized today, as many residents of nearby Rimrock, AZ rely on water flowing through the irrigation ditch for their gardens and livestock.

19) Tuzigoot National Monument

Crowning a desert hilltop is an ancient pueblo. From a rooftop a child scans the desert landscape for the arrival of traders, who are due any day now. What riches will they bring? What stories will they tell? Will all of them return? From the top of the Tuzigoot Pueblo it is easy to imagine such an important moment. Tuzigoot is an ancient village or pueblo built by a culture known as the Sinagua. The pueblo consisted of 110 rooms including second and third story structures. The first buildings were built around A.D. 1000. The Sinagua were agriculturalists with trade connections that spanned hundreds of miles. The people left the area around 1400. The site is currently comprised of 42 acres.

Tuzigoot National Monument is an 834-acre unit located just below the Mogollon Rim in Central Arizona. Currently, only 58 acres of the legislated amount are in National Park Service ownership. Although the climate is arid, with less than 12 inches of rainfall annually, several perennial streams thread their way from upland headwaters to the Verde Valley below, creating lush riparian ribbons of green against an otherwise parched landscape of juniper-dotted hills.

From the mineral-rich Black Hills to the south, to the red and white sandstone country of Sedona and the basalt-capped palisades of the Mogollon Rim to the north, to the limestone hills of the Verde Valley, the dynamic nature of the Earth's geologic processes is evident in the landforms surrounding the monument.

The monument contains numerous species of plants, such as mesquite, catclaw, and saltbush, which have adapted to life in an arid environment, but due to the microhabitats provided by the riparian corridor hosts populations of moisture-loving plants. The tall, large-leaved mesic species of trees, such as sycamore and cottonwood, found only in the riparian corridors, stand in stark contrast to the xeric species found on the neighboring lands. Nearby Tavasci Marsh, with its slow-moving water, provides yet another habitat for the great diversity of plant and animal life found within and adjacent to the monument.

Below - Tavasci Marsh

Tuzigoot Before Excavation
Caywood - 1934

20) Grand Canyon National Park

Welcome to Grand Canyon National Park! As you approach the Grand Canyon, you are crossing the Colorado Plateau, a 130,000 square mile bulge in the earth's surface spanning half of Utah and a good portion of Arizona, New Mexico, and Colorado. Around its edges are the upthrust Rocky Mountains, the stretched-apart Great Basin, the contorted rocks of Arizona's Transition Zone, and ancient volcanoes. Despite all the geologic activity around it, the plateau has managed to stay relatively flat and unfolded, but as a whole, it may have been uplifted nearly two miles.

It is the uplift and the down cutting that have created the canyon. About five to six million years ago, the Colorado River began to carve its way down through the domed region on its way to the sea. Like a knife slicing through a layer cake, the mile-deep river canyon exposed multi-hued layers of time; a geologist's dream come true. However, you don't have to be a geologist to appreciate the canyon's grandeur.

Erosion by wind, water, and gravity not only widened the canyon, it created an amazing variety of towers and spires, ridges and side canyons, shadows and highlights. The rainbow of rock colors is most intense in early morning or late afternoon light. If you are lucky, you will see a storm chase through the canyon casting shadows and mist as it goes.

Sightseers have been coming to view the wonders of the canyon since 1883. Prospectors soon found tourism more profitable than mining and built accommodations for them. One of the earliest visitors was Theodore Roosevelt, a lover of the West's wide-open spaces. He pushed for federal protection and in 1893, the area became a Forest Reserve. In 1908, it received a promotion to National Monument and in 1919, the National Park was authorized by Congress. The most recent upgrade was in 1975 when its boundaries were expanded, doubling its size.

As you enter the park, you'll receive a copy of the park newspaper, *The Guide*, from the National Park Service, which is a great source of information on restaurants, lodging, parking, ranger talks, activities and other guest services within or near the park. It includes maps, hours, prices, and other helpful information.

Waypoint Tours®

Plan, Enhance & Cherish
Your Travel Adventures!

This Waypoint Tour® is your
personal tour guide unlocking the
fascinating highlights, history,
geology & nature of
Sedona Arizona Red Rock Country.

Waypoint Tours® are entertaining,
educational, self-guided tours to help
plan your travel adventures,
enhance your travel experience &
cherish your travel memories.

Travel Destinations include:
Bryce Canyon UT
Grand Canyon South Rim AZ
Grand Canyon North Rim AZ
Grand Teton WY
Mt. McKinley Denali AK
Rocky Mountains CO
San Antonio & Missions TX
San Diego CA
San Francisco CA
Sedona Red Rock Country AZ
Washington DC
Yellowstone WY
Yosemite CA
Zion UT

DVD & CD Complete Tour Packages
DVD Tour Guides
DVD Tour Postcards
MP3 Downloadable Audio Tours
GPS Waypoint Tours® for iPhones +
Tour Guide Books Plus DVD & MP3s
Tour Road Guides Plus Audio CDs
Tour Guide Books

Waypoint Tours® Available Online at:
www.waypointtours.com
www.amazon.com
www.itunes.com

Highlights, History, Geology,
Nature & More!

Credits

Book by Waypoint Tours®
Photography by Waypoint Tours®
Original Tour Script by Bonnie Kline
& Laurie Ann, Editing by Laurie Ann
Monument Information by the National
Park Service, Maps by the Coconino
National Forest Service

Support Sedona Red Rock Country
with a membership or donation to:

Arizona Natural History Association
1824 S. Thompson St.
Flagstaff, AZ 86001
(928) 527-3450
http://www.aznaturalhistory.org/

National Forest Foundation
1824 S. Thompson St.
Flagstaff, AZ 86001
(928) 527-3600
http://www.nationalforests.org/explore/
forests/az/coconino

Photo Credits:
Pages 41, 42, 43 by the
National Park Service
Page 40 by Mark Rechtsteiner

T=Top, B=Bottom, R=Right, L=Left

Optional Audio CD Contents

Audio CD Driving Tour (45 min)

Optional DVD-ROM Contents

DVD Narrated Tour (45 min)
MP3 Audio Tour (45 min)
PC Multimedia Screensaver
Digital Photo Gallery

Breathtaking Photography,
Professional Narration &
Beautiful Orchestration

DVD Plays Worldwide in All Regions
DVD Mastered in HD in English
* Denotes Waypoints on DVD
PC Multimedia Screensaver &
Digital Photo Gallery Each Contain
30+ High-Resolution Photos

Professional Voicing by
Janet Ault & Mark Andrews
Recording Studio by Audiomakers
For private non-commercial use only
Detailed info & credits on
DVD-ROM

Optional Audio CD & DVD-ROM Info

Track #) Title

1) Sedona Arizona*
2) Bell Rock Vista*
3) Chapel of the Holy Cross*
4) Huckaby & Marg's Draw Trails*
5) Merry-Go-Round Formation*
6) Tlaquepaque Arts & Crafts Village*

Western Waypoints
7) Airport Mesa Vista*
8) Red Rock Crossing &
    Cathedral Rock*
9) Red Rock State Park*

Uptown & Northern Waypoints
10) Uptown Sedona*
11) Midgely Bridge*
12) Slide Rock State Park*
13) West Fork of Oak Creek*
14) Oak Creek Canyon Vista*

15) Grand Canyon National Park

Leave No Trace

Archaeological Site Etiquette Guide

Welcome to the past! The Coconino National Forest contains some of the nation's, and indeed the world's, greatest sites. Please take a few minutes to familiarize yourself with this guide which will facilitate an enjoyable visit for you and for others who follow you!

Archaeological sites on the Coconino National Forest are the remains of a long occupation of prehistoric, protohistoric, and historic cultures. They are a fragile and non-renewable resource. We are all stewards of these treasures. We must preserve these ruins for public enjoyment, education, and for their scientific values. The following will help minimize impacts to archaeological sites:

1. Walls are fragile and continue to deteriorate - that is why they're called ruins. Climbing, sitting, or standing on walls, picking up or moving rocks compromises these sites.
2. Artifacts, where they lay, tell a story. Once they are moved, a piece of the past is forever lost. Removing artifacts or piling them up in a site destroys the story they can tell.
3. Cultural deposits, including the soil on an archaeological site, are important for scientific tests used in reconstructing past environments, such as the kind of plants utilized by the inhabitants of long ago. Adding anything (such as offerings, etc.) to a site destroys the dating potential.
4. Fire destroys prehistoric organic materials and destroys the dating potential of artifacts. It also damages rock art by covering it with soot. Absolutely no fires, candles, smudging or smoking in sites. Camping is not allowed.
5. Drawing, scratching, carving, painting, and oil from even the cleanest hands can cause deterioration of the drawings. The dating potential is easily destroyed. Please assist those scientists trying to unravel the meaning of the symbols painted and pecked on stone. Refrain from touching the rock art. Mindless graffiti destroys rock art and is disrespectful to contemporary Native Americans.
6. Fragile desert plants and soils that are part of archaeological sites are destroyed when you stray from the trail. Also, snakes and other small desert animals make their homes in the bushes, under rocks and in burrows ... you may disturb them. Please stay on trails ... they are there for a reason. Bicycles and motorized vehicles are not allowed beyond the parking lot.
7. Animals damages sites by digging, urinating and defecating in them. They can destroy fragile cultural deposits and frighten other visitors. No pets allowed in these sites.

All archaeological and historic sites on the Coconino National Forest are protected by the Archaeological Resources Protection Act. These laws prohibit digging, removing artifacts, damage and defacement of archaeological resources on public lands, and provide felony and/or misdemeanor prosecution with imprisonment up to ten years and fines up to $100,000. If you see people vandalizing sites, please report it as soon as possible by calling the Coconino National Forest Fire Dispatcher's 24-hour line at 928-526-0600. By following these simple guidelines, YOU help preserve these unique and fragile remnants of OUR American heritage. Thanks for your cooperation, and we hope you enjoy your visit. Info provided by the Red Rock Ranger District - 928-282-4119.

Made in the USA
Coppell, TX
30 October 2022

85473513R00031